My First 18 Years

Raymond Beland

Bloomington, IN
authorHOUSE®
Milton Keynes, UK

AuthorHouse™
1663 Liberty Drive, Suite 200
Bloomington, IN 47403
www.authorhouse.com
Phone: 1-800-839-8640

AuthorHouse™ UK Ltd.
500 Avebury Boulevard
Central Milton Keynes, MK9 2BE
www.authorhouse.co.uk
Phone: 08001974150

First published by AuthorHouse 1/15/2007

ISBN: 978-1-4259-8276-8 (sc)

Library of Congress Control Number: 2006910761

Printed in the United States of America
Bloomington, Indiana

This book is printed on acid-free paper.

My First Day

(place new born picture here)

My New Born Information

full name________________________________

date of birth__________________time_________

day__________city____________state_________

country__________________________________

hospital______________clinic________________

doctor_______________mid wife______________

sex__________________weight_______________

length_______________blood type____________

hair color_____________eye color_____________

birth marks_______________________________

address__________________________________

____

phone number_____________________________

social security number_____________________

mothers name________________________________

mothers maiden name/surname_______________

fathers name_________________________________

grand parents name mother____________________

____

grand parents name father____________________

____

great grand parents names_____________________

____

sisters names_________________________________

brothers names_______________________________

pets names___________________________________

religion______________________________________

day care_____________________________________

1

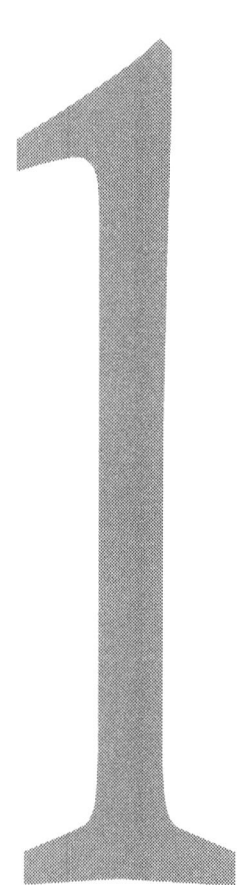

My First Birthday

(place first year picture here)

name ______________________________

address ______________________________

phone number ______________________________

nick name ______________________________

right or left handed ______________________________

height ______________ weight ______________

hair color ______________ eye color ______________

favorite toy ______________________________

first word ______________________________

favorite meal ______________________________

drink ______________________________

snack ______________________________

first tooth ______________________________

first step ______________________________

potty trained ______________________________

new sister or brother ______________________________

new cousins ______________________________

pets names ______________________________

illness or injury ___________________________

____

vacationed ______________________________

____

bereavements ___________________________

religion _________________________________

day care ________________________________

other:

____

____

____

____

____

____

2

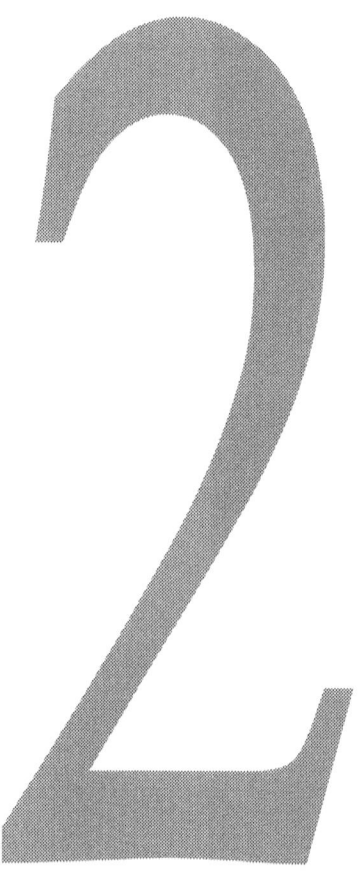

My Second Birthday

(place second year picture here)

name______________________________________

address____________________________________

phone number_______________________________

nick name__________________________________

height_____________________________________

weight_____________________________________

favorite T.V. show/movie___________________

favorite toy/game/sport____________________

favorite meal/drink/snack__________________

friends names______________________________

____

____

new sisters/brothers_______________________

new cousins________________________________

pets names_________________________________

illness/injuries______________________________

vacationed__________________________________

bereavements________________________________

religion_____________________________________

day care ____________________________________

other:

____

____

____

____

____

____

____

____

3

My Third Birthday

(place third year picture here)

name____

address_______________________________________

phone number__________________________________

nick name_____________________________________

height____

weight____

favorite T.V. show/movie______________________

favorite song/music___________________________

favorite toy/game/sport/team__________________

favorite meal/drink/snack_____________________

friends names_________________________________

____

____

new sisters/ brothers_________________________

new cousins___________________________________

pets names________________________________

illness/injuries____________________________

vacationed________________________________

bereavements______________________________

religion___________________________________

day care___________________________________

other:

____

____

____

____

____

____

____

4

My Fourth Birthday

(place fourth year picture here)

name____

address______________________________________

phone number_________________________________

nickname____________________________________

height______________________________________

weight______________________________________

favorite T.V. show/movie_______________________

favorite song/music___________________________

favorite toy/game/sport/team___________________

favorite meal/drink/snack______________________

friends names________________________________

new sisters/brothers___________________________

new cousins__________________________________

pets names___________________________________

pre-school/teacher_____________________________

illness____

injuries____

vacationed______________________________________

bereavements____________________________________

religion____

other:

____

____

____

____

____

____

____

____

5

My Fifth Birthday

(place fifth year picture here)

name______________________________________

address____________________________________

phone number_______________________________

nick name__________________________________

height_____________________________________

weight_____________________________________

favorite T.V. show/movie____________________

favorite song/music_________________________

favorite toy/game/sport/team_________________

favorite meal/drink/snack___________________

friends names_______________________________

new sister/brother__________________________

new cousins_________________________________

pets names__________________________________

kinder garden/teacher_______________________

lost first tooth________________________________

grew new secondary tooth______________________

illness/injuries________________________________

vacationed____________________________________

bereavements__________________________________

religion_______________________________________

hobbies_______________________________________

other:

____

____

____

____

____

____

6

My Sixth Birthday

(place sixth year picture here)

name___________________________________

address_________________________________

phone number___________________________

e-mail address__________________________

my space address________________________

nickname_______________________________

height__________________________________

weight__________________________________

favorite T.V. show/movie__________________

favorite song/music______________________

play an instrument_______________________

favorite toy/game/sport/team______________

favorite meal/drink/snack_________________

friends names___________________________

new sister/brother_______________________

pets names________________________________

first grade school/ teachers____________________

lost first tooth______________________________

grew new secondary tooth____________________

illness/injuries_____________________________

vacationed_________________________________

bereavements_______________________________

religion____________________________________

hobbies____________________________________

other:

____

____

____

____

7

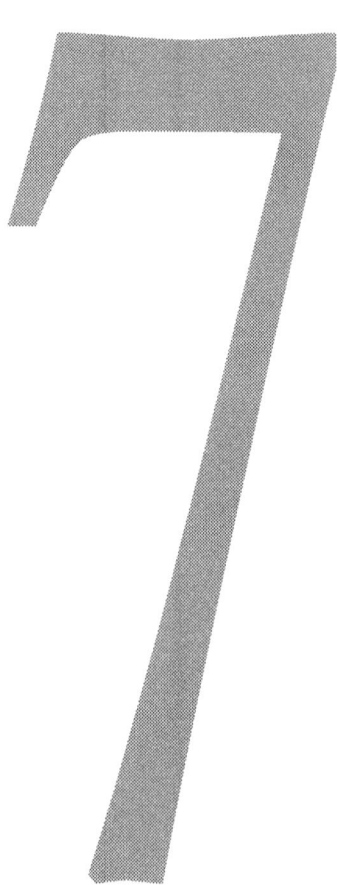

My Seventh Birthday

(place seventh year picture here)

name_______________________________________

address_____________________________________

phone number________________________________

e-mail address_______________________________

my space address_____________________________

nick name___________________________________

height______________________________________

weight______________________________________

favorite T.V. show/movie______________________

favorite song/music__________________________

play an instrument___________________________

favorite game/sport/team_____________________

favorite meal/drink/snack_____________________

friends names_______________________________

new sister/brother____________________________

new cousins________________________________

pets names_________________________________

second grade school/teacher___________________

illness/injuries______________________________

vacationed_________________________________

bereavements_______________________________

religion____________________________________

hobbies____________________________________

other:

____

____

____

____

____

8

My Eighth Birthday

(place eighth year picture here)

name____

address______________________________________

phone number________________________________

e-mail address________________________________

my space address______________________________

nick name_____________________________________

height_______________________________________

weight_______________________________________

favorite T.V. show/movie_______________________

favorite song/music___________________________

play an instrument____________________________

favorite game/sport/team______________________

favorite meal/drink/snack_____________________

friends names_________________________________

new sister/brother_____________________________

new cousins______________________________

pets names______________________________

third grade school/teachers________________

illness/injuries___________________________

vacationed______________________________

bereavements____________________________

religion_________________________________

hobbies_________________________________

other:

____

____

____

____

____

9

Ninth Birthday

(place ninth year picture here)

name______________________________________

address____________________________________

phone number_______________________________

e-mail address______________________________

my space address____________________________

nick name__________________________________

height_____________________________________

weight_____________________________________

favorite T.V. show/movie______________________

favorite song/music__________________________

play an instrument___________________________

favorite game/sport/team_____________________

favorite meal/drink/snack_____________________

friends names_______________________________

new sister/brother____________________________

new cousins_______________________________

pets names________________________________

fourth grade school/teachers_________________

illness/injuries_____________________________

vacationed_________________________________

bereavements_______________________________

religion____________________________________

hobbies____________________________________

other:

____

____

____

____

____

10

Tenth Birthday

(place tenth year picture here)

name____

address______________________________________

phone number_________________________________

e-mail address_______________________________

my space address_____________________________

nick name____________________________________

height_______________________________________

weight_______________________________________

favorite T.V. show/movie_____________________

favorite song/music__________________________

play an instrument___________________________

favorite game/sport/team_____________________

favorite meal/drink/snack____________________

friends names________________________________

new sister/brother___________________________

new cousins________________________________

pets names_________________________________

fifth grade school/ teachers_____________________

illness/injuries______________________________

vacationed_________________________________

bereavements_______________________________

religion___________________________________

hobbies___________________________________

other:

____

____

____

____

____

11

Eleventh Birthday

(place eleventh year picture here)

name___________________________________

address________________________________

phone number___________________________

e-mail address__________________________

my space address________________________

nick name______________________________

height_________________________________

weight_________________________________

favorite T.V. show/movie_________________

favorite song/music______________________

play an instrument_______________________

favorite game/sport/team_________________

favorite meal/drink/snack________________

friends names___________________________

new sister/brother_______________________

new cousins________________________________

pets names_________________________________

sixth grade school/teachers__________________

illness/injuries_____________________________

vacationed_________________________________

bereavements_______________________________

religion____________________________________

hobbies____________________________________

other:

____

____

____

____

____

12

Twelfth Birthday

(place twelfth year picture here)

name________________________________

address______________________________

phone number__________________________

e-mail address_________________________

my space address________________________

nick name____________________________

height_______________________________

weight_______________________________

favorite T.V. show/movie__________________

favorite song/music______________________

play an instrument_______________________

favorite game/sport/ team_________________

favorite meal/drink/snack_________________

friends names__________________________

new sister/brother_______________________

new cousins________________________________

pets names_________________________________

seventh grade school/teachers________________

illness/injuries______________________________

vacationed__________________________________

bereavements________________________________

religion_____________________________________

hobbies_____________________________________

other:

____

____

____

____

____

13

Thirteenth Birthday

(place thirteenth year picture here)

name________________________________

address________________________________

phone number__________________________

e-mail address__________________________

my space address________________________

nick name______________________________

height_________________________________

weight_________________________________

favorite T.V. show/movie___________________

favorite song/music_______________________

play an instrument________________________

favorite game/sport/team__________________

favorite meal/drink/snack__________________

friends names___________________________

new sister/brother________________________

new cousins______________________________

pets names_______________________________

eighth grade school/teachers_________________

illness/injuries____________________________

vacationed_______________________________

bereavements_____________________________

religion_________________________________

hobbies_________________________________

other:

14

Fourteenth Birthday

(place fourteenth year picture here)

name________________________________

address______________________________

phone number_________________________

e-mail address_________________________

my space address_______________________

nick name____________________________

height_______________________________

weight_______________________________

favorite T.V. show/movie__________________

favorite song/ music_____________________

play an instrument______________________

favorite game/sport/team_________________

favorite meal/drink/snack_________________

friends names__________________________

new sister/brother______________________

new cousins________________________________

pets names_________________________________

ninth grade school/teachers____________________

illness/injuries______________________________

vacationed_________________________________

bereavements_______________________________

religion____________________________________

hobbies____________________________________

other:

____

____

____

____

____

15

Fifteenth Birthday

(place fifteenth year picture here)

name____

address______________________________________

phone number_________________________________

e-mail address________________________________

my space address______________________________

nick name____________________________________

height_______________________________________

weight_______________________________________

favorite T.V. show/movie_______________________

favorite song/music___________________________

play an instrument____________________________

favorite game/sport/team______________________

favorite meal/drink/snack______________________

friends names________________________________

new sister/brother____________________________

new cousins________________________________

pets names_________________________________

tenth grade school/teachers____________________

illness/injuries______________________________

vacationed__________________________________

bereavements_______________________________

religion____________________________________

hobbies____________________________________

other:

____

____

____

____

____

16

Sixteenth Birthday

(place sixteenth year picture)

name____

address______________________________________

phone number_________________________________

e-mail address________________________________

my space address_____________________________

nick name____________________________________

height_______________________________________

weight_______________________________________

favorite T.V. show/movie_______________________

favorite song/music___________________________

play an instrument____________________________

favorite game/sport/team______________________

favorite meal/drink/snack______________________

friends names_________________________________

new sister/brother_____________________________

new cousins______________________________

pets names______________________________

eleventh grade school/teachers_______________

illness/injuries___________________________

vacationed______________________________

bereavements____________________________

religion_________________________________

hobbies_________________________________

other:

17

Seventeenth Birthday

(place seventeenth year picture here)

name______________________________________

address____________________________________

phone number_______________________________

e-mail address_____________________________

my space address___________________________

nick name__________________________________

height_____________________________________

weight_____________________________________

favorite T.V. show/movie___________________

favorite song/music________________________

play an instrument_________________________

favorite game/sport/team___________________

favorite meal/drink/snack__________________

friends names______________________________

new sister/brother_________________________

new cousins________________________________

pets names_________________________________

twelfth grade school/teachers_______________

college plans_______________________________

illness/injuries_____________________________

vacationed_________________________________

bereavements_______________________________

religion____________________________________

hobbies____________________________________

other:

____

____

____

____

18

Eighteenth Birthday

(place eighteenth year picture here)

name____

address______________________________________

phone number_________________________________

e-mail address_______________________________

my space address_____________________________

nick name____________________________________

height_______________________________________

weight_______________________________________

favorite T.V. show/movie_____________________

favorite song/music__________________________

play an instrument___________________________

favorite game/sport/team_____________________

favorite meal/drink/snack____________________

friends names________________________________

new sister/brother___________________________

new cousins________________________________

pets names_________________________________

formal education___________________________

career move________________________________

girl friend/boyfriend______________________

illness/injuries___________________________

vacationed_________________________________

bereavements_______________________________

religion___________________________________

hobbies____________________________________

other:

____

____

____

Never stop setting goals and dreaming big!
Be safe and enjoy your life!

www.ingramcontent.com/pod-product-compliance
Lightning Source LLC
Chambersburg PA
CBHW021234280526
45784CB00005B/2099